BARCLAY BUTERA

MODERN LIVING

BARCLAY BUTERA
MODERN LIVING

GIBBS SMITH
TO ENRICH AND INSPIRE HUMANKIND

TO MY STAFF

I truly appreciate the support and dedication you have given me over

the years. You are all like family to me, and the fun along with the

hard work has made this journey one that has well exceeded even my

greatest dreams! Thank you for all that you do.

With much love, Barclay

16 17 18 19 20   5 4 3 2 1

Text © 2016 by Barclay Butera
Photograph credits on page 198

Published by
Gibbs Smith
P.O. Box 667
Layton, Utah 84041

1.800.835.4993 orders
www.gibbs-smith.com

Designed by Rita Sowins/Sowins Design
Pages produced by Virginia Brimhall Snow
Printed and bound in Hong Kong

Gibbs Smith books are printed on either recycled, 100% post-consumer waste, FSC-
certified papers or on paper produced from sustainable PEFC-certified forest/controlled
wood source. Learn more at www.pefc.org.

Library of Congress Control Number: 2015949762
ISBN 9781423642220

CONTENTS

INTRODUCTION

Today's modern living is about so much more than simply surrounding one-self with the sleekest, streamlined furnishings and the most avant-garde design. It's edited, comfortable, and effortless. I believe this distinctive style to be a true study in contradiction—where traditional antiques and outspoken contemporary pieces seamlessly mix together in blissful harmony, where laid-back cool meets formal elegance, where rustic and weathered collides with sophisticated and refined, but most of all, where the expected merges with the unexpected. This integrating of styles is never thematic—nothing is "on display" and everything has a sense of purpose. Color, texture, proportion, and fabrics are all important but versatility is key. As a result the design embodies a fresh and timeless element keeping it from ever feeling ordinary or dated.

After spending the past several decades of my life designing enviable spaces for my discerning clients, I have seen more than my fair share of fads and trends come and go. Through the years, I have found that striking a balance between what is beautiful and what is practical is the one design philosophy that always stands the test of time. Regardless of the home's architecture, the style of furnishings, the art collection, or even the arrangement of lighting and accessories, if I am able to create a comfortable environment for my client that is as stylish and inviting as it is functional and true to their character then no matter how many times their taste may change—and it will—the home will always remain true to how they live.

So whether my client is a successful businessman coming to me to design a majestic mountain retreat, a hip bachelor in need of a polished pad, or a young couple with children ready to build their family's dream home, it is my goal to create a space that perfectly suits their needs, where they can welcome friends and loved ones eagerly and often, all the while surrounded with the right furnishings to make them feel right at home. For me, that is the very definition of modern living.

CITY
CREEK

Just a short drive down the canyon from my design showroom in Park City, Utah, lies a new development called City Creek Center that has created quite a buzz in the local community. Located right in the heart of Salt Lake City, it features upscale retail shops and dining destinations alongside high-rise residential living and office space. With a placid winding creek running through it, manicured tree-lined walkways, and an open-air mall with a retractable glass roof, it has given the downtown area a much needed modern makeover. Just to the south of the main shopping area is the Regent Building, one of the sleek and inspiring residential towers located in the Center. When the developers approached me to design their Sky Suite Model, I was eager to become a part of a project that helped to revitalize a city and breathe new life into the local economy.

Bold, bright, and convenient, I found my inspiration for the design of this urban high-rise in both the old and the new architectural landmarks it overlooks. Thanks to an assortment of perfectly imperfect vintage pieces found at local flea markets, tribal rugs, and stylish mid-century modern furnishings this apartment became an eclectic medley of antique and avant-garde. Rich ruby, citrine, and emerald jewel tones establish a warm energy, feeling at once fresh and nostalgic while mixed metals give the space a dose of luster and shine. By purposefully avoiding color or wallpaper, it became easy to capitalize on the outstanding views of the city skyline and the peaks of the Rocky Mountains just beyond. The outcome is an apartment that perfectly embodies a blend of polish and glamour with hip downtown cool.

FACING: A rich color palette, sleek wood paneled fireplace, and elegant furniture define this eye-catching living room with a balanced sense of traditional and contemporary qualities.

ABOVE: A pair of sleek metal-framed chairs lend a straightforward industrial look to the space as well as a convenient spot to lounge while taking in the dazzling view of the city's night skyline.

ABOVE: The uncluttered office has a spacious feel, while a metal-framed desk and upholstered curved-back chair give the room a striking, glamorous note.

FACING: Large windows flood the interior in natural light and a well-appointed settee provides the perfect lookout spot to take in the view of the city and the mountains just beyond.

FACING: Crisp white cotton sheeting engulfs the bed while floor-to-ceiling drapery panels can be drawn for privacy or pulled back to showcase the spectacular view.

ABOVE: A brilliant emerald green and gold chest is paired with a stunning round mirror in the home's entry making a chic statement and setting the tone for the home's sophisticated decor.

KINGS
ROAD

Envisioning a home where their children could run around barefoot, where she could cook gourmet meals in a state-of-the-art kitchen and where they could entertain friends and relatives in a casual yet elegant environment, our young clients set out to build their family's dream home on the coast of Southern California. A referral from one of our previous clients, this couple came to us with a very clear vision of what they wanted: an industrial modern home that would seamlessly balance her love of antiques with his affinity for more contemporary-looking pieces all the while being a family-friendly space where their kids could roam free. No small task but my design team and I were eager to design a home for them that reconciled stylish living with the realities of having a growing family.

As huge fans of reclaimed wood long before it became a widespread trend, our clients wanted this to be the foundation for the design. We paired this rustic and organic element with a restrained color palette to create a home that is clean-lined and modern but at the same time warm and welcoming. This juxtaposition of style continued throughout the home when we combined an extraordinarily elegant Italian chandelier with a rustic farm-style dining table and then inserted cleverly placed shells and beach relics throughout the home in a nod to its coastal locale. Despite the utilitarian needs of the residence, we made sure that family treasures were given pride of place. By transforming personal photographs into triptych panels of wall art and incorporating much-loved family heirlooms into the design, my team and I were able to keep the balance of old and new, and by doing so we were able to create a home that our clients and their family can love, live, and laugh in together for many years to come.

ABOVE: A luxurious blend of soft linens, velvets, and suedes in a neutral color palette complement the reclaimed wood elements throughout the space and beautifully contrast the dark tone of the wallpaper.

FACING: Large sliding glass paneled doors flood the seating group in the living room with natural light while providing easy access to the outdoor patio and expansive ocean view.

FACING: By incorporating custom upholstered side chairs in a soft neutral color,
the dining room style is elevated to one
of chic sophistication.

ABOVE: A stunning waterfall chandelier
above the dining space exudes a heavy
dose of glam while the distressed
farmhouse-style dining table below it
adds to the home's overall warm and
inviting atmosphere.

ABOVE: The glass-door cabinet provides space for unique treasures and mementos as well as a convenient spot to store kitchen essentials including glassware and serving pieces.

FACING: Here stainless steel appliances pop against the muted hand-rubbed finish of the cabinetry and a pair of well-placed barstools offer both form and function to the kitchen's centerpiece: a custom crafted island with ample amounts of storage.

ABOVE: Weathered-looking custom millwork with brushed nickel hardware and a herringbone-patterned fireplace screen combine to add a unique and stylish twist to this cozy living space.

FACING: Mismatched leather wing chairs, a black lacquered desk, and a collection of vintage world maps come together to make an impactful statement in this sophisticated office setting.

ABOVE: A well-lit hallway leads into the stunning guest bath where a spa-like oasis awaits.

FACING: The use of weathered reclaimed wood extends to the bathroom where frosted glass globe pendants illuminate the space with a soft glow.

"MY DESIGN TEAM AND I WERE EAGER TO DESIGN A HOME FOR THEM THAT RECONCILED STYLISH LIVING WITH THE REALITIES OF HAVING A GROWING FAMILY."

String globe lights and perfectly placed candlelit hurricanes create the ideal lighting combination to enhance the dusk time harbor view of this cozy outdoor patio space.

ALPINE LANE

Located in the majestic Northern Rockies, Sun Valley, Idaho is home to some of the most picturesque terrain in the country. Surrounded by jaw-dropping peaks and an immense blue sky, our client has always felt there is something truly magical about this town; when deciding where to build his picture-perfect winter getaway, it stood out as the obvious choice. Being a successful business mogul and a dynamic father to four grown children, he wanted this home to be a place where he and his family could get together to ski, escape their busy lives, and spend uninterrupted time together. Having already designed several homes for this client, my design team and I were inspired to create this property to be a stunning mountain retreat that balances his affinity for both rustic and modern living.

After a lengthy ground-up construction process, the spacious home finally came together conveying a warm and inviting tone with an extra level of sophistication not often encountered in a space that is centered around the wintry pursuits of skiing, snowboarding, and sledding. In an effort to emphasize the home's streamlined architecture, we utilized clean, fresh furniture pieces and layered in unique vintage items with patina to add character. Instead of using a lot of bold colors to energize the space, we went with a neutral base and then injected color strategically—mostly in the form of artwork, rugs, and textiles. The house is also enlivened with a wide array of texture and pattern: bamboo window shades, nail head–studded upholstery and various natural wood finishes all feel appropriate to the setting without falling into cliché. The end result was a chic, comfortable home where my client and his family could relax and simply enjoy life together in a cozy and intimate setting.

"INSTEAD OF
USING A LOT OF
BOLD COLORS
TO ENERGIZE
THE SPACE, WE
WENT WITH A
NEUTRAL COLOR
BASE AND THEN
INJECTED COLOR
STRATEGICALLY."

In the home's main living space, natural elements pair with modern furnishings and a subdued palette creating a warm and inviting space to take in the panoramic mountain vistas.

FACING: Gold sheathed hurricanes work in tandem with other sculptural lighting fixtures to create a warm and inviting ambiance throughout the game room.

ABOVE: Warm neutral tones displayed in the built-in bookcases, the upholstered sofa, and the lounge chairs transition into the throw pillows and even the accessories.

Cool metal touches combine with wood finishes to give this home a sophisticated air. The cabinet and drawer pulls, the sink hardware, even the kitchen appliances are all coated in a sleek metallic tone.

ABOVE: Staggered windows in the wall above the staircase allow for doses of natural light to peek through and create a unique spot to display a collection of vintage equestrian models.

FACING: The sweeping limestone-capped staircase brings a sense of drama to the rustic stone-faced entry of the home, while a clean-lined settee adds a touch of modern elegance.

FACING: The expansive floor-to-ceiling windows in this inviting master bedroom allow for unobstructed views and create a space of effortless ease and relaxation.

ABOVE: A vintage-looking horse painting over the bed successfully unifies the warm brown and gold accents in this comfortable guest bedroom retreat.

ABOVE: Leather drawer pulls, petrified wood sculptures, and a woven tray all come together to add a rustic and textural element to the space.

FACING: Vintage framed photographs of the city offer a sense of charm to this otherwise sophisticated bedroom suite.

"[WE] WERE INSPIRED TO CREATE THIS PROPERTY TO BE A STUNNING MOUNTAIN RETREAT THAT BALANCES HIS AFFINITY FOR BOTH RUSTIC AND MODERN LIVING."

The indoor pool and spa allow for a dip even on the coldest of winter days while the stylish chaise lounge chairs on the picturesque outdoor patio provide the ideal place to recline, unwind, and enjoy the crisp mountain air.

ABOVE: The perfect place to entertain friends or enjoy a meal al fresco, this exquisite deck boasts a dining area where pewter-accented dinnerware adds a touch of panache to the warm teak outdoor furniture.

FACING: Simple glass hurricanes flank a branch-filled vase on this casual outdoor tablescape elevating the surrounding natural beauty.

CORAL STONE

After becoming acquainted with a charismatic builder in Park City, Utah—where one of my three design showrooms is located—we began collaborating on a number of projects together and quickly developed a solid working relationship. When he became involved in a project building custom luxury homes on a golf course just outside of Palm Springs and needed a designer to do the models, I was his first call. The residences of the Andalusia community in La Quinta, California, are a collection of homes that are centered on delivering the modern-day desert lifestyle: sliding glass-panel doors give the sense of indoor/outdoor living, expansive patios and private courtyards provide ample space for entertaining, and custom-designed pools allow for a refreshing reprieve from the desert heat. When it came to decorating the model, it was my goal to create a home where anyone who walked in could easily imagine themselves living there.

The Mediterranean-style home's open and spacious floor plan is ultimately what inspired my restrained design of the space, which was a departure for me. I knew that an abundance of patterned wallpaper, layered textiles and a heavy-handed use of accessories would not work here so my team and I kept to a decidedly mid-century modern foundation. We focused on incorporating a variety of textures and shapes that combined to create compelling compositions from every angle. The walls were purposefully kept stark white to establish a blank canvas that we punctuated with saturated abstract artwork and colorful upholstered pieces while a few well-placed metallic accents added a sleek jolt to the interior. The end result is a lighthearted and relaxing environment that embodies a fresh and vibrant take on desert design.

ABOVE: With layers of palm trees, lush plants, and a lounge-worthy pool deck, this back yard is overflowing with desert appeal.

FACING: A modern pool with simple, clean lines brings a sleek, minimalist look to the unique indoor/outdoor living element of this house.

FACING: Anchored by the quartz-stacked stone fireplace, this color-neutral living room is defined by linear and geometric elements that embody the home's modern luxe style.

ABOVE: Expansive polished porcelain floors unify the kitchen and dining space while a grey and white chevron area rug ties together the color scheme.

ABOVE: There is an effortless transition from the bedroom to the adjacent sitting area, where the bold color story continues and is punctuated by abstract art, a cowhide rug, and modern inspired furnishings.

FACING: Bursts of cool blues and bright yellows, a cozy fireplace, and lively patterns entertain the eye in this stylish bedroom suite.

GREY STONE

When I was approached to design a second model for the Andalusia custom home project in La Quinta, California, I wanted to do something distinctly different from the first—I set out to create a serene environment that would merge the rustic beauty of the desert and the peaceful serenity of the coast. With the community being situated at the base of the breathtaking Santa Rosa Mountains but only a few hours' drive from the relaxing beaches of Southern California, it seemed like the perfect way to showcase the home's unique quality of easy modern living. Having owned homes in both Palm Springs and Newport Beach myself, I felt if anyone could seamlessly bring together the best that these two worlds have to offer, it was me.

Because of the abundance of windows throughout the space and the panel of disappearing glass that unified the living and dining areas with the adjacent patio, the home seemed to always be awash in natural light giving it a warm and inviting feel. I wanted to play this up by sticking to a very fresh but muted color palette. Combining soft blue tones with a base of creamy neutrals and whites, my team and I transformed the interior into a place that feels cool and refreshing despite the blazing temperatures outside. My strategy for achieving a cohesive desert/beach look was to generate a blend of visual texture and striking patterns. We did this by incorporating pieces that have both a traditional and current feel: a striped rug mixes with floral throw pillows and animal prints while contemporary art is paired with furniture in more transitional silhouettes. The outcome was a home that, according to the sales manager, anyone who came through to tour it would exclaim: Oh, I could live here!

ABOVE: The rectangular elements of the dining room and the arched window work together to draw the eye to the scenic desert oasis just beyond.

FACING: With such a smooth indoor to outdoor transition, it is difficult to tell where the open and airy living room ends and where the picturesque patio begins, making this outdoor space a true extension of the home.

"I TRANSFORMED
THE INTERIOR INTO
A PLACE THAT
FEELS COOL AND
REFRESHING DESPITE
THE BLAZING
TEMPERATURES
OUTSIDE."

Classic white subway tile sets the
stage for a kitchen centered around
entertaining while the open floor plan
gives the home a bright and airy feel.

ABOVE: A large oval-shaped soaking tub and polished nickel hardware play up the cool tones of the bathroom and are modern yet timeless additions to the luxurious space.

FACING: Glass and metallic accents combine to complement the soothing pale blue and neutral tones of the master bedroom while a large glass-paneled sliding door allows for a generous view of the majestic desert scenery.

VICTORY RANCH

Nestled amongst the rolling foothills of Utah's pristine backcountry, the custom cabin-style estates of Victory Ranch set a new benchmark for rustic luxury living. With sweeping views of the rugged Wasatch Range and the calming waters of the Jordanelle Reservoir in the valley below, the dramatic beauty of this private residential community is unmatched. Each of these secluded homes is surrounded by nothing but wide open terrain as far as the eye can see—whether it be the grassy green fairways of the eighteen-hole golf course, the dozens of rural hiking and biking trails, or the flowing rivers perfect for endless days of fly fishing. Come winter, bikes and fishing poles are exchanged for skis and snow shoes since the community is just a stone's throw from the world-class skiing of neighboring Park City and Deer Valley resorts, making this development the ideal place to truly connect with the great outdoors throughout the year.

When you walk into the model my team and I designed for Victory Ranch, it's easy to forget that you're in the open wilderness of the rural Utah backcountry—and that's just the idea. I wanted to create a chic yet casual atmosphere by utilizing materials common in mountain homes while also introducing very modern and industrial elements. The soaring glass windows and beautiful beams of local reclaimed wood are the bones of the sanctuary while the metal collar ties, concrete counter tops, and steel strap detailing on the fireplace set the tone for a more urban ambiance. With uninterrupted scenic outlooks from every room, I maintained the warmth of the space by layering a variety of textures and roughhewn finds including hair-on-hide benches, distressed leather lounge chairs, fur throws, and horned accessories. By combining these elements with a muted color palette and low profile seating, the seamless marriage of traditional and contemporary continues resulting in a unique and inspiring setting perfect for taking in all the natural beauty that abounds.

FACING: An open rustic-meets-modern style kitchen combines weathered grey and white hues with reclaimed wood and stainless steel appliances for a clean and simple finish.

ABOVE: Despite the fact that it is part of the open floor plan, the dining room still feels comfortable and intimate with the use of slipcovered chairs, a round table, and a soothing color palette.

ABOVE: Brushed limestone countertops and unique steel and wood barstools pick up the charcoal grey accents found throughout the home and lend an industrial feel to the kitchen.

FACING: Equestrian-inspired artwork, a weathered console, and cowhide cubes come together to deliver a design that is at once cohesive and inviting.

FACING: This bathroom is both stylish and practical with cool grey and white hues, clean lines, and sleek hardware.

ABOVE: A reclaimed wood-paneled wall provides an unexpectedly unique backdrop for a luxuriously modern free-standing soaking tub.

FACING: The cleverly placed wood stag head continues the rustic theme and when combined with a fur blanket it provides a natural element of texture to the space.

ABOVE: Wood and iron framed beds, cozy plaid wool blankets, and a pair of plush over-sized bean bags come together here in this bunk room to embody the spirit of ranch living.

GARNET AVENUE

Oftentimes, new chapters in life bring on an inexplicable desire for a change of scenery. Such was the case with our client when the last of her three children had gone off to college and she decided it was finally time to downsize and simplify her life. Making the move from her spacious traditional home in Calabasas, California to a scaled-back waterfront bungalow located on the scenic Balboa Island, she had found her dream property. It was here that she could spend endless carefree days at the beach, paddle boarding around the bay to her heart's content and truly enjoying the company of her family and nine grandchildren. Eager to transform this downsized space into a chic and modern take on coastal living, she paid my design team and me a visit at our Newport Beach showroom to gain some inspiration.

Because we had worked with her on her two previous homes, we knew that this particular client was never wishy-washy when it came to making decisions. It came as no surprise when she walked into the showroom just days after we had unveiled our new contemporary nautical look and decided on the spot that she wanted us to replicate this design for her in her new home. The bright and airy floor plan was the perfect backdrop for this striking color palette featuring bold blue and white patterns with tangy punches of tangerine. When mixed with the bleached oak wood floors, high ceilings and loft windows, the space became a vivid and inviting environment that was everything she had hoped for. By far, our client's favorite hangout is the waterfront patio complete with a fire pit and made all the more enticing by a pair of comfy outdoor sofas piled high with brightly patterned pillows. The perfect spot to sit back and revel in her newfound life of ease.

ABOVE: Sophisticated decor with a coastal flair is just the right touch in this charming seagrass-lined built-in cabinet.

FACING: One of the first spaces you see when entering the home, this colorful living room is a bright and welcoming spot to lounge after a long day at the beach.

FACING: The gorgeous white tongue and groove-paneled ceiling adds textural contrast to the home's bright, open nature while uniting the kitchen, dining room, and living room spaces.

ABOVE: Just off the kitchen, a comfortable patio is the picture-perfect spot to dine al fresco and enjoy the warm ocean breeze.

FACING: A pair of French doors leading to a sun-drenched patio allows plenty of natural light to flood the master bedroom, making it a bright, cheery place to spend time.

ABOVE: A bold blue and white palette with plenty of seashell accessories thrown in adds to the home's coastal vibe.

HUMBOLDT AVENUE

Just one hundred miles east of Los Angeles and nestled in the Coachella Valley, lies the hidden gem of the desert: a city called La Quinta. When our client was deciding on a location where she and her family could retreat to from the icy cold winters of Colorado, a custom residence in La Quinta's exclusive Madison Club—where the temperature rarely deviates from the eighty degrees Fahrenheit mark—was just what she was looking for. With its quiet neighborhoods filled with handsome villas and a luxury world-class golf course that would satisfy her husband's penchant for the game, this community is the modern interpretation of California's classic country club living.

There were many reasons why we immediately hit it off with this client from the moment we met her. Like me, she possesses an unabashed love of art and bold pops of color, she is not afraid to make daring pattern choices and together we share a deep affection for dachshunds, both of us owning a pair. At our initial meeting she arrived wearing a very brightly colored silk and beaded tunic and announced that she wanted it to be our inspiration when designing her home. She and her husband were not look-ing for the stereotypical Palm Springs home—no walls of glass, no low-slung roof lines, and no sleek mid-century décor. Instead, they wanted a home that was inspired by the natural environment and that would take full advantage of the spectacular desert views. By layering classic archways and carved wood detailing with brilliant jewel tones, bold stripes and bright ikat prints, my team and I were able to create a chic desert oasis where our clients would love to entertain friends, and retreat to weekend after weekend.

FACING: Bold jewel tones and bright ikat prints enliven the neutral walls and seating area while vaulted ceilings and large glass-paneled sliding doors expand the space for an open and airy feel.

ABOVE: This dining area, just off the kitchen, perfectly embodies the very definition of refined elegance, and the glamorous chandelier hanging above it only adds to the air of sophistication.

"SHE ARRIVED WEARING A VERY BRIGHTLY COLORED SILK AND BEADED TUNIC AND ANNOUNCED THAT SHE WANTED IT TO BE OUR INSPIRATION WHEN DESIGNING HER HOME."

The playful print on the wood-framed barstools adds a touch of whimsy to the otherwise polished and sophisticated kitchen. Custom cabinetry with intricate woodcarvings and a pair of iron lanterns hanging over the expansive marble-top island round out the refined look.

FACING: An oversized tufted head-board and a vaulted ceiling accented by rich wood beams work in tandem to draw the eye up adding a dramatic feel to the luxurious master bedroom.

ABOVE: The comfortable chaise adjacent to the fireplace makes for a warm, cozy spot to relax on a chilly desert night.

ABOVE: Here, an antique cabriole leg desk punctuates this smart office nook while an oversized linen lounge chair beckons to be curled up in with a blanket and a book.

FACING: Silk drapery panels, a tailored striped bench, and layers of throw pillows give this guest bedroom an upscale elegance that is both warm and inviting.

WHITE PINE CANYON

Once we had completed two projects for our Newport Beach clients—one at the waterfront Balboa Bay Residences overlooking Newport Beach's famous harbor and the other in the exclusive Bayshores beach community just off Pacific Coast Highway—they decided it was time to try their hand at mountain living where big skies and rural landscape dictate the scene. They stumbled across a property nestled in the hillside of Park City, Utah that captured both their hearts and their imagination so they snapped it up and entrusted my design team and I with the task of turning it into a mountain estate that would seamlessly merge their desire for a home in a rustic locale with their love for luxe modern living.

After months of renovations on the expansive 18,000 square foot property, we knew that for these clients and their two college-age sons, comfort was key. It was only fitting that we centered our design around a variety of textures that would create a sense of warmth and coziness to each of the rooms in their spacious home. Soft velvets and plush cashmeres were paired with rich faux furs and distressed stamped leather hides all set against a decidedly neutral color palette. While the interior boasts traditional bones with the arched hallways and the dark mahogany wood paneling, the sleek unexpected silhouettes of the furnishings and the stylish lighting fixtures are anything but conventional. These elements along with a few handcrafted designs and an ever-growing collection of vintage pieces balance the striking combination of old and new. For our clients this became a home where they can gather with friends, enjoy the great outdoors, or just stay inside and soak up the comfort.

ABOVE: The classic and timeless architecture of the arched hallway is underscored by the dark wood paneling, while contemporary artworks add an unexpected touch.

FACING: Though warm and inviting, the home also possesses a dramatic quality thanks to the soaring ceilings, extensive millwork, and incredible floor-to-ceiling windows.

FACING: Continuing a classic-meets-modern theme, contemporary globe pendant lights hang over sleek leather barstools and provide a striking pop of contrast against an otherwise traditional kitchen.

ABOVE: A dramatic chandelier draws the eye up and makes for an elegant statement above the rustic leather chairs in this cozy fireside seating area.

"THE SLEEK
UNEXPECTED
SILHOUETTES OF
THE FURNISHINGS
AND THE STYLISH
LIGHTING FIXTURES
ARE ANYTHING BUT
CONVENTIONAL."

A mix of traditional and modern,
classic furnishings and architectural
details are paired with a sleek marble
slab fireplace and striking abstract art.

ABOVE: Rich wood tones, a plush angular sectional sofa, and an abundance of plaid and chocolate throw pillows instill this living room with a sense of rustic luxury. The stacked stone fireplace adds the finishing touch.

FACING: The wide open floor plan allows for a great mix of patterns and textures to come together to create one cohesive, stylish space.

FACING: Glass globe pendant lights illuminate the entertaining bar and work in tandem with the smoky-glass chandelier to spotlight the room's intriguing mix of materials and architectural elements.

ABOVE: A mixture of classic and modern style unites in this stylish dining room, making for a comfortable and inviting space to gather.

ABOVE: Here, a pair of matching over-sized lounge chairs and ottomans in a sumptuous cream velvet echo the bedroom's muted color scheme while a luxe chandelier serves as a dramatic focal point.

FACING: Large wood-framed windows in the master suite flood the room with natural light and offer spectacular views of the breathtaking mountain terrain that surrounds the home.

ABOVE: The woodsy view, along with the subtle color palette and the organic elements, all come together to keep the mood of this guest bathroom both elegant and earthy.

FACING: A soft neutral palette, metallic accents, and a marble-top vanity elevate the design of this posh powder bath.

MONTAGE DEER VALLEY

Tucked away amongst the aspens, firs, and rugged vistas of the Wasatch Range, lies the private condominium residences of the Montage Deer Valley. These craftsman-style retreats, located on the upper floors of the hotel, boast breathtaking panoramic views and exclusive ski-in/ski-out access to the adjacent Deer Valley resort. Several of these vacation homes were offered as fully furnished residences where luxury interior designers from around the country were asked to showcase their updated interpretation of a classic and timeless lodge getaway. I was invited to curate a two-bedroom residence where I felt inspired to infuse the space with a sophisticated and tailored take on modern mountain living.

Featuring high ceilings, dramatic roof lines, and expansive windows, this retreat is awe-inspiring. In an effort to allow the vibrant colors of the scenery take center stage, I kept to an almost exclusively neutral color palette throughout the interior. By layering in luxurious textures from shearling rugs to felted wools and distressed leathers with whipstitch detailing, I was able to capture a casual but refined atmosphere while dark wood flooring and cabinets offered a more polished air. Combinations of sleek upholstered seating, structured wood pieces, and metallic elements punctuated every room creating a modern elegance that was warm and stylish but most of all, inviting. The homeowners who ended up buying this unit loved the design so much, they kept everything just as we had designed it, and did not change a thing.

ABOVE: A modern glass-top table with simple, clean lines brings a sleek, minimalist look to this stylish dining space.

FACING: Low-profile furnishings, a clean palette, and sleek lines set the tone for the home's contemporary design style.

ABOVE: The abstract artwork and the clean lines of the furnishings stand in stark contrast to the home's rustic setting.

FACING: A polished wood-and-leather tufted bed serves as the focal point in this sleek and stylish master bedroom while a pair of swanky curved-back chairs add to the room's sense of sophistication.

TERRANEA RESORT

After seeing how I was able to transform the interiors of the L'Auberge Del Mar into a fresh, new standard of coastal hospitality, I was contacted by the resort executives at Terranea to breathe new life into the sales model for their custom vacation homes. Located on the majestic cliffs of the Palos Verdes peninsula and just minutes from downtown Los Angeles, Terranea is a luxury waterfront resort that includes a collection of residential bungalows, casitas, and villas available for purchase. Thrilled at being asked to redesign the showcase ocean golf villa, which sits just a stone's throw from the resort's award-winning golf course, I set out to bring the natural beauty of the home's surroundings to the indoors.

With sweeping vistas of the golf course's sixth hole and the Pacific Ocean, I drew my inspiration for the home's design from the effortless nature of seaside living. Enriched with Mediterranean architecture, modern conveniences, and the natural beauty of the 102-acre coastal setting, I kept to a palette of soft blues, crisp whites and lavish greys. The art and the accessories throughout the residence are a reflection of the oceanfront locale: the sculptural chunks of coral, the framed sea fans and metallic shells as well as abstract wall art that speaks to the colors of the sea. However, the most amazing feature of this home is that no matter what room you are in, you are only steps from being outside. Whether it's through a set of French doors in the kitchen that lead you to the backyard or through an arched doorway in the bedroom that opens up to a private courtyard, every room has an access point to the beauty of the outdoors making it the coastal sanctuary that dreams are made of.

ABOVE: An easy transition through the French doors to the outdoor patio gives the space an essence of privacy and exclusivity.

FACING: This private courtyard filled with succulents and palms is the perfect place to start the day, reading the morning paper and sipping a cup of coffee.

FACING: The living and dining spaces come together to set the scene with calming blue and white tones and subtle beachy elements.

ABOVE: Pillared archways section off the kitchen and breakfast nook from the rest of the open floor plan in a unique and unexpected way.

ABOVE: A simple orchid arrangement is paired with a sunburst mirror and other accessories to bring life into the space and evoke a sophisticated feel.

FACING: Here, a mixture of both traditional and modern design elements create a stylish and welcoming dining room.

FACING: Framed sea fans play up the blue and white palette used throughout the entire suite and offer an interesting focal point on the guest bedroom wall.

ABOVE: Classic furnishings and contemporary art combine in this relaxing guest suite where dark wood tones are brightened by soft blues and creamy neutrals.

CAGNEY LANE

When one of our most beloved long-time clients came to us asking that we design a polished bachelor pad for her son in a two-bedroom residence located just off the Pacific Coast Highway, we jumped at the opportunity to create a masculine and modern take on beach living. Because this was his first time living on his own, we felt it was very important to design the space to be a true representation of her son's personality, but at the same time push him to make unique selections that he would not normally pick out on his own. In doing so, we were able to design a home that is a masterful blend of sleek sophistication and boyish charm.

Because the original home was reminiscent of a dark and gloomy smoker's den, my design team and I deemed it necessary to strip it down to the studs and do a full-scale remodel. Once we had a blank canvas to work with, we infused the space with a heavy dose of rich wood paneling, brushed steel accents and contemporary lighting fixtures. The leather wallpaper paired with muted velvet and silk textiles set a warm tone for the space while the cool mix of contemporary art and textured throw pillows added the perfect dash of color. In a nod to his love of cars (and his hair color), the Ferrari-red lacquered oven added the punch of energy we needed to give the space just the right amount of character. I believe every home needs a statement piece like this to truly create a connection with the owner, and make it feel as though it is one of a kind.

ABOVE: A cooled-down color palette paired with weathered dark oak flooring sets the tone in the home's sleek entry space.

FACING: The tufted leather headboard in rich chocolate leather creates a stylish backdrop and adds a masculine touch to this sophisticated master bathroom.

QUARRY MOUNTAIN

For our East Coast-based clients, Utah was just a scenic vacation destination where they spent time during the holidays and while on ski trips with their family every year—that is, until they decided to pick up and move across the country with their three young children and two dogs to make it their permanent residence. They immediately fell in love with an estate in one of Park City's most sought-after neighborhoods: Quarry Mountain Ranch. Situated in a pristine meadow that was once a dairy farm, the craftsman-style residence is surrounded by a bucolic landscape of private lakes, pine-covered mountain peaks, and fields of wild grass. Loft-like timber trusses and stacked stone pillars lend a sculptural quality to the exterior unifying the home's modern rustic architecture while the interior floor plan lends itself to comfortable and harmonious family living.

What began as a simple kitchen remodel quickly snowballed into a full-scale renovation of the entire property after I did a walk through with our clients and made a few suggestions on what I thought needed updating in order to make the home a more livable space. The traditional wainscoting walls and heavily varnished wood floors in the main living space were exchanged for sleek white walls and European oak floors stained in a matte ebony finish to retain the organic quality of the wood. Bedrooms were given a light and airy tone, punctuated with clean-lined furnishings and soothing textures while the media room and study were reenergized in a warmer, more rustic tone with nature-inspired wallpaper, faux fur pillows, and heavily patterned upholstered pieces. The kitchen was given new life with sleek quartz countertops and custom cabinetry that combines an understated contemporary design with a weathered-looking finish. After all was said and done, this modernized mountain home is everything our clients imagined it to be—peaceful, warm, and luxurious but most importantly, it is a breath of fresh air.

ABOVE: The vibrant sectional boasts a sleek design with elegant nail head detailing while overstuffed throw pillows in various textures and patterns serve to add comfort and contrast to the space.

FACING: With plenty of seating, a billiards table, a wet bar, and even a popcorn maker—this game room is the perfect place for entertaining family and friends.

ABOVE: A grouping of distressed leather lounge chairs with oversized nail head trim work creates a cozy conversation area.

FACING: Here in this intimate gathering space, rustic meets chic with the stylish combination of unexpected patterns and textures.

"BEDROOMS WERE
GIVEN A LIGHT
AND AIRY TONE,
PUNCTUATED WITH
CLEAN-LINED
FURNISHINGS AND
SOOTHING TEXTURES."

Spacious and luxurious with soft fabrics and a calming color palette, this master bedroom is a decadent space designed for relaxation.

TABLE ROCK DRIVE

When our Los Angeles-based clients decided they needed a place where they could go to get a break from the everyday hustle and bustle of city life, they looked south to the stunning cliffs of Laguna Beach. The charm and tranquility of this slow-paced beach town made it the ideal locale for their much-needed vacation retreat. With only one item on their list of must-haves for the home—a jaw-dropping ocean view—they began their search. After several months of looking without any luck, they finally found a home that gave them the stunning panoramic views of the Pacific Ocean they wanted, but it was extremely outdated and in need of a complete renovation. My design team and I were excited and eager to help them transform this home into their idyllic modern beach getaway.

The vision for this home was to have it effortlessly blend contemporary elements with its natural surroundings; we wanted to bring the beach indoors but in a fresh and unique way. To accomplish this we combined sun-bleached hardwood floors, perfect for hiding traces from sandy feet, with panels of floor to ceiling windows making it hard to tell where the interiors end and the shoreline begins. A neutral color palette of soft linens and seagrass wallpaper extends throughout the home but is broken up by splashes of aqua blues and celadon greens creating a calming spa-like atmosphere. This serene color palette paired with a dose of modern wood pieces, statement mirrors, and enviable lighting fixtures provides the space with an understated yet elegant allure fitting for the design-loving homeowners to relax in and truly unwind.

ABOVE: A show-stopping constellation mirror above the clean-lined console table rounds out the modern and so-phisticated look of the living room.

FACING: Soft neutrals combine with calming shades of blue in a nod to the relaxing and tranquil style of living on the coast, while metallic finishes add a luxe quality to the space.

FACING: The living room opens to the dining area, where full-length floor-to-ceiling glass sliders offer jaw-dropping views of the Laguna Beach coastline.

ABOVE: Clean lines paired with chrome accents and marble counter-tops; this kitchen exudes a polished and luxurious look.

ABOVE: A simple but elegant wood-framed linen bed layered with posh pillows contributes to the comfortable spa-like atmosphere.

FACING: The bleached hardwood flooring continues into the master suite where it combines with the soothing celadon walls and anchors the serene design aesthetic.

GLENEAGLES DRIVE

Not every project my design team and I take on is a full-scale remodel. Oftentimes, we have clients come to us after purchasing a home and living there for several months only to realize that the space and its furnishings are not at all conducive to their family's needs. Such was the case with our client in Newport Beach, California who came to us as a referral from a local carpenter whom we had worked with on several projects in the past. Their property had such great architectural details but it left much to be desired when it came to the design details. By making some simple updates to the interior space and furnishings, we were able to help our client transform her home into a polished, yet family-friendly haven full of style and character.

One of my favorite features of the home was the existing hardwood flooring that ran throughout the entire first level. In some rooms it was a beautiful basket weave design and in others it was planks of various widths and sizes but either way it was stunning. When we paired it with the addition of crisp white wall paneling and glossy molding details, it created the perfect backdrop for a home based on combining the old with the new. After merging new furniture pieces and accessories with our client's existing pieces, the renovated space became a medley of styles and influences. The addition of streamlined upholstery in a fresh and modern palette of soft greys and celadon blues only worked to enhance the traditional sophistication of our client's treasured items. The end result is a home that merges stylish living with the reality that there are no rules when it comes to surrounding yourself with the things that you love.

ABOVE: A traditional crystal chandelier, hand-painted silver leaf walls, and timeless French doors complete the look of the home's classic, tailored design.

FACING: Here in the living room, a muted palette and a wide range of textures and materials—linen, velvet, silk, glass, metallic, and polished wood—create depth and visual interest.

ABOVE: Just off the kitchen, the dining area is a bright, open space with stylish mixed seating inspiring a chic and sophisticated atmosphere.

FACING: The glossy X-base trestle table adds a modern twist to the traditional design while the polished nickel nail head on the upholstered dining chairs provides a dose of glamorous style to the space.

FACING: In a room defined by soft curves and muted tones, the rich mahogany cocktail table offers clean, sharp lines and brings an unexpected modern element to the space.

ABOVE: In the office, a coffered ceiling and built-in bookcases offers the perfect backdrop to display a collection of sports memorabilia and other treasured belongings.

WILSHIRE

I n need of a Los Angeles pied-à-terre, my long-time client found just what he was looking for in a historical 1930s building with stunning architectural design located on the famed Wilshire corridor. This eight-unit chateau boasts leaded-glass windows, dramatic turrets and lush landscaped gardens, giving the impression that it belongs in the rolling hills of the French countryside rather than the streets of a busy urban city. In an effort to pay homage to the unique history of this property, I felt inspired to design it with a sense of style and glamour synonymous with the iconic golden age of Hollywood but at the same time, infuse it with an updated modern aesthetic suitable for everyday living.

Perhaps most notable upon entering the residence is the refined air of sophistication. Immersed in a soft palette of creamy neutrals, warm chocolates, and sumptuous camels, the living room feels at once chic and inviting. The soaring vaulted ceilings and bright open floor plan of this prewar residence proved to be the perfect backdrop for my client's enviable art collection while richly toned hardwood floors keep the space grounded, and art deco–inspired lighting fixtures add a dramatic flair. With such a limited space, I felt it was important that each element in the design evoke a sense of purpose without feeling overwhelming. Subtle Greek key drapery trims layer harmoniously with textured silks and a plush velvet pinstriped sofa combines with a graphic houndstooth rug delivering a masculine touch of haberdashery. Glossy low-slung furnishings with modern lines pair with crystal and gold accessories to add a sense of polished informality all coming together to create a home that is a lesson in livable elegance.

ABOVE: The tiled backsplash and a few small framed pieces of art provide the needed punch of color that stands in contrast to the kitchen's pared-down palette.

FACING: The limited square footage of the space makes it all the more important to incorporate pieces with a sense of purpose. Cubes and ottomans allow for additional seating options while tiered wood pieces create the perfect landing spot for stacks of coffee table books.

ABOVE: A glass-coated beach print and a bamboo window shade break up the otherwise urban sensibility of the master bath.

FACING: Here the various rich textures of the pillows, bedding, and draperies come together to add depth to the bedroom's monochromatic color palette.

ACKNOWLEDGMENTS

A special thanks to:
Kerry Freimann
Gary and Mary Lisenbee
Dave Wilson and Jimmy Ruscitto of Sun Valley, Idaho

PHOTO CREDITS

LORI BRYSTAN STUDIOS

Author headshot, 2

CRAIG DIMOND (courtesy of City Creek Development)

City Creek, 12

DAVID JOHNSON AND JILL YOUNG, HEADWATERS INTEGRATED MARKETING

Coralstone, 58–67

Greystone, 68–75

MARK LOHMAN

Kings Road, 20–37

Garnet Avenue, 88–101

Humboldt Avenue, 102–111

White Pine Canyon, 112–127

Montage Deer Valley, 128–135

Terranea Resort, 136–147

Cagney Lane, 148–153

Table Rock Drive, 176–183

Gleneagles Drive, 184–191

Wilshire, 192–197

JOSHUA R. WELLS

Alpine Lane, 38–57

SCOT ZIMMERMAN

City Creek, 10, 13–19

Victory Ranch, 76–87

Quarry Mountain, 154–175

Barclay Butera Interiors delivers the capabilities of an international interior design firm with the personal touch of a boutique showroom. The enterprise is comprised of full-service interior design capabilities, over 20 professional interior designers on staff, and three featured showrooms in Newport Beach, California, West Hollywood, California, and Park City, Utah. The website offers an extensive online shopping experience, including Barclay Butera Private Collections and personally selected curated vendors from around the world.

The Barclay Butera Private Collections represent Butera's iconic designs incorporated with the products of some of the most recognized licensed partners in the industry: Bradburn Gallery Home lighting; Eastern Accents luxury bedding, decorative pillows, down, and mattresses; Highland House furniture; Kravet textiles and carpets; Leftbank Art; Mirror Image Home decorative mirrors; Mirth Studio handcrafted wood flooring; Nourison carpets; and Winfield Thybony wallcoverings.

He has appeared on NBC's *Today Show*, *Extra!*, CBS, ABC, Fox, *Beautiful Homes & Great Estates*, and HGTV; he has received press in the *New York Times*, *New York Post*, *Los Angeles Times*, *Wall Street Journal*, *House Beautiful*, *Traditional Home*, *Veranda*, *House & Garden*, *Elle Decor*, *Luxe Interiors + Design*, *Town & Country*, *Robb Report*, and *Esquire*.

BARCLAY BUTERA
SHOWROOMS

BARCLAY BUTERA INTERIORS

WEST HOLLYWOOD
918 North La Cienega Boulevard
West Hollywood, California 90069
TEL 310.432.4252

NEWPORT BEACH
1745 Westcliff Drive
Newport Beach, California 92660
TEL 949.650.8570

PARK CITY
255 Heber Avenue
Park City, Utah 84060
TEL 435.649.5540

WWW.BARCLAYBUTERA.COM